D0848629

Capybaras

by Grace Hansen

Abdo
SUPER SPECIES
Kids

abdopublishing.com

Published by Abdo Kids, a division of ABDO, PO Box 398166, Minneapolis, Minnesota 55439.

Copyright © 2017 by Abdo Consulting Group, Inc. International copyrights reserved in all countries. No part of this book may be reproduced in any form without written permission from the publisher.

Printed in the United States of America, North Mankato, Minnesota.

052016

092016

 THIS BOOK CONTAINS RECYCLED MATERIALS

Photo Credits: Animals Animals, iStock, Science Source, Shutterstock

Production Contributors: Teddy Borth, Jennie Forsberg, Grace Hansen

Design Contributors: Laura Mitchell, Dorothy Toth

Cataloging-in-Publication Data

Names: Hansen, Grace, author.

Title: Capybaras / by Grace Hansen.

Description: Minneapolis, MN : Abdo Kids, [2017] | Series: Super species |
    Includes bibliographical references and index.

Identifiers: LCCN 2015959226 | ISBN 9781680805437 (lib. bdg.) |
    ISBN 9781680805994 (ebook) | ISBN 9781680806557 (Read-to-me ebook)

Subjects: LCSH: Capybara--Juvenile literature.

Classification: DDC 599.35--dc23

LC record available at http://lccn.loc.gov/2015959226

Table of Contents

Giant Rodents!

Capybaras are the largest rodent **species**. The next largest rodent is the beaver.

Capybaras can weigh up to 175 pounds (80 kg). That is about the same as 3 beavers!

Capybaras can grow just over 2 feet (61 cm) tall. That is the same height as a standard poodle. Capybaras grow up to 4 feet (122 cm) long.

2 ft

4 ft

2 ft

9

Body

Capybaras are covered in brown hair. Some can be reddish or gray in color. They have small ears and long faces.

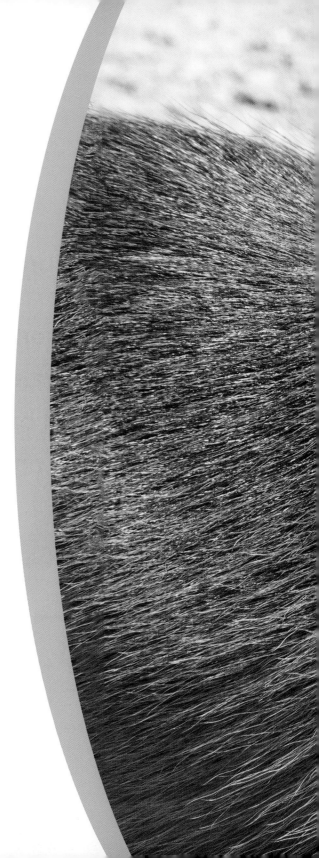

11

Capybaras have long, sharp teeth. They use their teeth for eating grass. They especially like eating water plants.

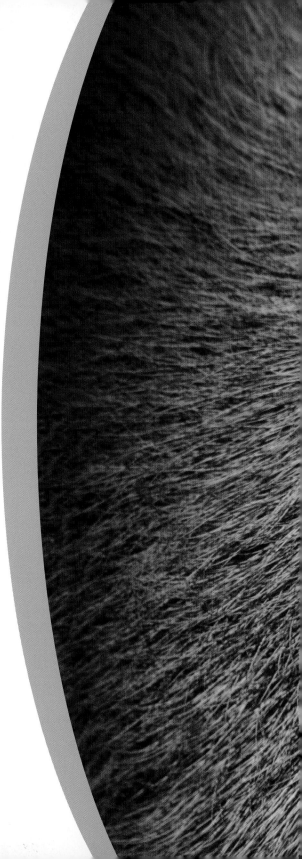

13

Capybara Life

Capybaras spend lots
of time near and in water.
Their **webbed** feet make
them good swimmers.

14

15

Capybaras live in Central and South America. It can get very hot. Sitting in water keeps them cool.

Capybaras even make big noises! They yelp, bark, and chirp. They also growl and purr to **communicate**.

Baby capybaras are called pups. Around 5 pups are born at once. Pups weigh up to 3 pounds (1.4 kg) at birth. But they grow fast!

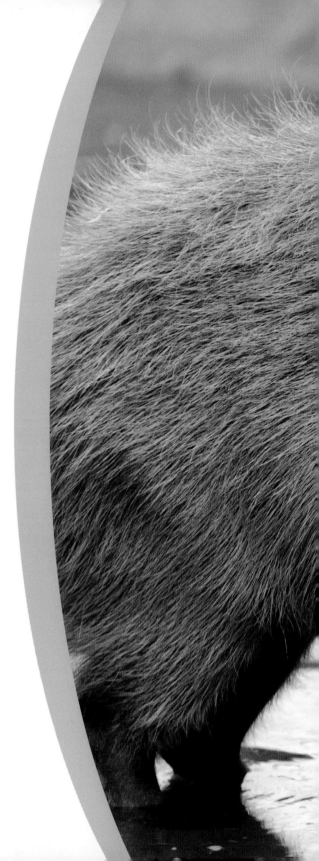

More Facts

- Capybaras usually live in groups of up to 20 individuals.

- A capybara's nostrils, eyes, and ears are on the top of its head. If a capybara is scared, it can hide in the water. It sticks the top of its head out of the water to breathe. It can also watch and listen until it is safe to go back to land.

- Capybaras live 8 to 10 years in the wild.

Glossary

communicate – to share or exchange information.

species – a particular group of animals that are similar and can make young animals.

webbed – having toes connected by skin tissue.

Index

abdokids.com

Use this code to log on to abdokids.com and access crafts, games, videos, and more!

Abdo Kids Code:
SCK5437